D1042648

Books in The Tuttle Twins series:

The Tuttle Twins Learn About the Law
The Tuttle Twins and the Miraculous Pencil
The Tuttle Twins and the Creature from Jekyll Island
The Tuttle Twins and the Food Truck Fiasco
The Tuttle Twins and the Road to Surfdom
The Tuttle Twins and the Golden Rule
The Tuttle Twins and the Search for Atlas
The Tuttle Twins and their Spectacular Show Business

Find them all at TuttleTwins.com

© 2016 Connor Boyack
All rights reserved.

No graphic, visual, electronic, film, microfilm, tape recording, or any other means may be used to reproduce in any form, without prior written permission of the author, except in the case of brief passages embodied in critical reviews and articles.

ISBN 978-1-943521-05-0

Boyack, Connor, author.
Stanfield, Elijah, illustrator.
The Tuttle Twins and the Food Truck Fiasco / Connor Boyack.

Cover design by Elijah Stanfield
Edited and typeset by Connor Boyack

Printed in the United States

10 9 8 7

THE TUTTLE TWINS
and the
FOOD TRUCK FIASCO

Regulations
for Portable Food Vendors

CONNOR BOYACK

Illustrated by Elijah Stanfield

This book is dedicated to
Ralph Smeed.

Making statism unpopular,
through billboards and books.

"Pull over, everybody!" Emily shouted as she waved a large sign in the air so passing drivers could see what she and Ethan were selling.

The Tuttle twins had been running a lemonade stand for a few months. On hot, sunny days more people would stop for a refreshing drink, but on cooler days, like today, there was less interest.

Ethan was getting bored—and drinking too much of their lemonade. "What? I'm thirsty!" he said to Emily as she frowned at him in disapproval.

Cars had been driving right by them all afternoon, and the twins were beginning to wonder if it was time to close down for the day.

Just then, Emily spotted a bright green truck. "Hey, Amy's here!" she said as the truck came to a stop.

Amy's family lived down the street from the Tuttles. "Just what I'm in the mood for!" she said, exiting her truck. "Can I buy a cup?"

"The cups are free, but you can buy some lemonade," Ethan replied, chuckling loudly.

Emily handed Amy her cup of lemonade in exchange for two quarters. "Could we look inside your food truck?" she asked Amy. "I've always wanted to see what it's like."

"You bet!" Amy said. "It's like a kitchen on wheels."

She let them explore the truck as she heated up a couple slices of leftover pizza for them.

Ethan was very curious and had lots of questions about Amy's business. "This is your job?" he asked. "How do you find all your customers?"

"With this truck, I can go where the customers are," Amy told them. "For example, a bunch of food trucks will be at the football game this Saturday."

"Our family loves to go to football games!" Emily said excitedly. "We are big Tigers fans."

Ethan's mouth was full of Amy's macaroni and hot dog pizza, so he simply nodded in agreement.

"Then maybe I'll see you there!" Amy said, waving goodbye. As she drove off, another customer stopped by for some lemonade.

It wasn't hard for the twins to convince their parents to take them to the game that Saturday afternoon.

"There are so many food trucks!" said Mrs. Tuttle as they pulled into the parking lot. The family was excited to get some yummy lunch before the game.

Emily smiled as she looked around—there were so many different trucks with colorful designs and delicious smells.

"I'm going to get some tacos," Mr. Tuttle said. He handed some money to the twins.

Mrs. Tuttle decided to try a bacon cheeseburger. "Let's meet up when we all have our food," she said as she started toward a silly looking truck that was half cow, half pig.

"There's Amy's truck!" Ethan shouted, pulling on Emily's arm. Emily had been talking all day about how great Amy's pizza was.

The twins ran through the crowd to get a few slices to eat.

The twins had to wait in line; Amy's food truck was pretty popular. While they waited, they noticed a big "FOR SALE" sign on the side of the truck.

"Amy, why are you selling your food truck?" asked Ethan once it was their turn. "I thought you really liked your job."

Amy's smile quickly disappeared, and she became sad. "I really wish I could keep doing it, but I'm not making enough money," she replied.

The twins were confused. "But there are lots of people buying your pizza," Ethan said. "So what's the problem?"

"Well, the laws in our city make it really hard to own a food truck business that's *profitable*—meaning, that it makes more money than it costs to operate."

Amy showed the twins a paper that listed all of the laws food trucks had to follow.

"I have no idea why there are so many *regulations*," she said, "but these rules are to blame for putting me out of business."

"I just learned that one of the laws won't let me bake my fresh dough unless I buy a really expensive oven, like the ones in a normal restaurant," Amy added. "It would cost way too much money to put one inside my truck!"

"Doesn't your kitchen work fine the way it is?" Ethan asked. "Why would they make a law like that?"

As Amy shrugged her shoulders, Emily pointed to the neighboring food truck. "Maybe one of the other food truck owners knows," she said.

The twins borrowed the paper from Amy and approached a food truck selling Thai food.

"Excuse me, may we ask you a question about this?" Ethan asked the owner. The man next to her suddenly got very angry and shouted some words in his native language that didn't sound very nice.

"Please excuse my husband," the woman said. "We work very hard to provide for our family, but these laws might put us out of business!"

She explained that they felt it was unfair to require food trucks to obey all these extra regulations when normal restaurants didn't have to.

"I'll tell you why that is," called out a man from another food truck who had overheard them. "The guy who owns all the Bob's Big BBQ restaurants is good friends with the Mayor. It's *protectionism!*"

The twins walked toward the man, who also sold barbecue. "What do you mean?" asked Emily curiously. "What is protectionism?"

"I can make better food than Bob, and for a better price," he said. "Of course, Bob doesn't like that, so he got his friends in government to make laws that protect his business by making it more difficult for mine. *That* is protectionism."

Blue and red lights flashed suddenly. The crowd made way for a police car that stopped in front of the taco truck where Mr. Tuttle was. The police officer said that all the food trucks had to leave once the game was over, and never return.

"But nobody has complained!" protested the taco truck's owner. "Nobody has gotten sick or had any problems with my food."

"I'm just doing my job," said the police officer. "If you don't like the law, try to get the city council to change it," he said.

The police officer handed out a new paper with a new law saying that food trucks couldn't sell food within 2,000 feet of a restaurant. That meant no selling at the stadium, since it was close to Bob's Big BBQ.

"That doesn't seem fair," Mr. Tuttle remarked. "The food truck owners are just trying to make an honest living. They aren't hurting anyone."

"But the city council and its laws *are* hurting people," said a young man nearby. "I'm Jared. I actually own three of these food trucks."

"You own three food trucks?" said Mrs. Tuttle, who sounded surprised. "You seem very young to be so successful."

"That's the real beauty of the food truck business," Jared explained. "People like me who start out with very little *capital*—that's a fancy word for money— can't afford to buy or build a traditional restaurant."

"But because a food truck costs less than a building," he said, "I can offer great food for a better price than the big restaurants."

"That's called *competition*," Mr. Tuttle explained to the twins. "Each business tries hard to make the best food for the lowest price, in order to get more customers and make more money."

"Exactly!" Jared replied. "My first priority is to keep customers happy and safe," he explained. "If my prices are too high, or if customers don't like my food, they will go somewhere else."

"But the worst thing to happen would be if my food made someone sick. They would tell their friends and my business would suffer."

Amy's Crazy Pizza

BANG BANG Noodles

REAL PINKY'S BARBECUE

UNIQUE FOODS

FAST SERVICE

LOW PRICES

MANY MENU OPTIONS

NO SURPRISES

COMFORTABLE ATMOSPHERE

Bob's BIG BBQ

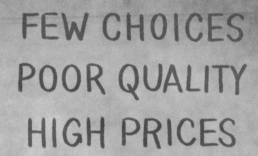

"As food trucks attract more customers, restaurants like Bob's Big BBQ become less popular," Jared continued. "But instead of lowering his prices or making better food, Bob uses protectionist laws to beat his competition. Without competition, Bob can sell lower quality food at higher prices, and people wouldn't have much of a choice. These laws are really bad for customers."

Mrs. Tuttle also pointed out that the government often claims these laws protect customers. "But they actually just help Bob's Big BBQ," she said.

"That's right," Jared replied, smiling. "I need to care for my customers in order to stay in business—that's why I pay experts to test the cleanliness of my trucks and the quality of the food. My food is healthier and safer than what you might buy in many restaurants," he added. "I don't need the city council to tell me how to run my food trucks."

"We shouldn't have to follow these unfair rules or pay extra fees," he said, pointing to the other food trucks.

"But... wouldn't it bother you that you'd be breaking the law?" Emily wondered.

"Look, we're all Tigers fans here, right?" Jared asked. "Imagine if the referee was a fan of the other team, and he made the Tigers play by harder rules, so that his favorite team won."

"That would be unfair," Emily said.

"Exactly," Jared replied. "But we wouldn't blame our team—we'd blame the cheating referees!"

"It's the same thing with the food trucks," he continued. "The city council is hurting businesses like mine in order to help the other team win—in this case, restaurants like Bob's Big BBQ."

After enjoying the football game, the Tuttles walked back outside where they heard some horns honking. The food trucks were driving away from the stadium to follow the police officer's orders.

"Don't worry about us—we'll manage even with this new law," Jared told the family.

Suddenly, Ethan remembered what the police officer had said earlier. "Hey, what if we could get the law changed?" he wondered aloud.

Jared looked skeptical. "Good luck with that…" he said, waving goodbye to the Tuttle family. "If you could somehow make that happen, you would be our heroes."

Ethan and Emily didn't know how to change the law. Who would they have to talk to? How long would it take? Would it be hard? The twins asked themselves many questions as the Tuttle family returned home.

That evening, the twins asked their dad to help them come up with a plan. Mr. Tuttle had worked on some *political campaigns* when he was younger, helping change laws and get people elected to the city council—so he had lots of suggestions for the twins.

The three of them thought up lots of ideas they could try, and Mr. Tuttle wrote everything on the whiteboard in his office.

"To change these food truck laws, you have to educate people," he explained. "And to do that, you have to get their attention."

Soon, the plan was complete—the twins had an idea they felt would get people's attention, and get them to pressure the city's Mayor and council into changing the law.

The twins spent the next several days planning for their event, Food Truck Friday—calling each food truck owner and designing flyers to help spread the word.

Jared and Amy came over to help, and brought green T-shirts and buttons for their friends and customers to wear to show their support.

Mr. Tuttle's job was to call reporters and editors at the news stations and tell them about what would be happening.

When they learned that a couple of nine-year-old children were planning a protest, reporters seemed very interested in coming to the event.

When Food Truck Friday arrived, dozens of trucks began parking near the football stadium. Ethan and Emily also set up their lemonade stand.

More than a hundred people arrived, enticed by the offer of big discounts on delicious food.

The twins handed out T-shirts to anybody who wanted one, and soon the crowd looked like a sea of neon green.

TV crews set up their cameras, and a crowd of people gathered by the stage.

"I didn't have to shut my business down because of spoiled food or a lack of customers," Amy told the reporters. "It was because of this piece of paper!" she said, holding up the list of food truck regulations passed by the city council.

"Look around you," she continued. "All of these people are happily buying and selling. Nobody is getting sick. People are choosing what they want to do. This is freedom!"

Jared then stepped forward to speak. "What the public needs to understand is that this freedom comes at a cost. Each of these food truck owners is breaking a law today—but it's an unfair one."

The cameras zoomed in on the paper where Jared was pointing to the new law that said, "No food truck may operate within 2,000 feet of a restaurant."

"There is no reason to force our businesses to stay away from restaurants, except to protect them from competition. Protectionism is wrong!" Jared shouted.

"That's why we're here!" Ethan said loudly. All the reporters turned around to listen to the twins. "We discovered that Bob, who owns this restaurant, was able to get the Mayor to pass this law as a way to shut down his competition."

"So we brought the competition straight to his doorstep!" Emily said with a big grin.

A large, white car suddenly screeched to a halt across the street, and its driver threw open the door.

"Get out of here, all of you!" the driver bellowed, as the TV cameras turned toward him.

It was Bob, the restaurant's owner, and he was really upset!

"You're violating the law," Bob said to Ethan and Emily. "I'm going to call the police!" he shouted, waving his finger at the twins.

The reporters were wide-eyed and amazed that they were catching this on camera. It certainly didn't look good for Bob to show him yelling at young children on TV!

"Don't worry guys, I doubt the police will come today," Jared whispered to the twins. "It wouldn't look very good for the Mayor if the police were to shut us down now."

Jared was right; Bob didn't even bother calling the police, but instead went inside his restaurant to hide from the cameras.

That night, all of the local TV stations showed Bob's angry rant along with an interview of Ethan and Emily explaining why they wanted the law to be changed.

The next morning, the city newspaper featured the story on its front page.

The Tuttle family's phone was ringing off the hook with friends, family, and neighbors excited to see that Food Truck Friday was such a success.

"But we're not done yet," Ethan and Emily told each of the people who called. They made sure to invite them to the next part of the project.

43

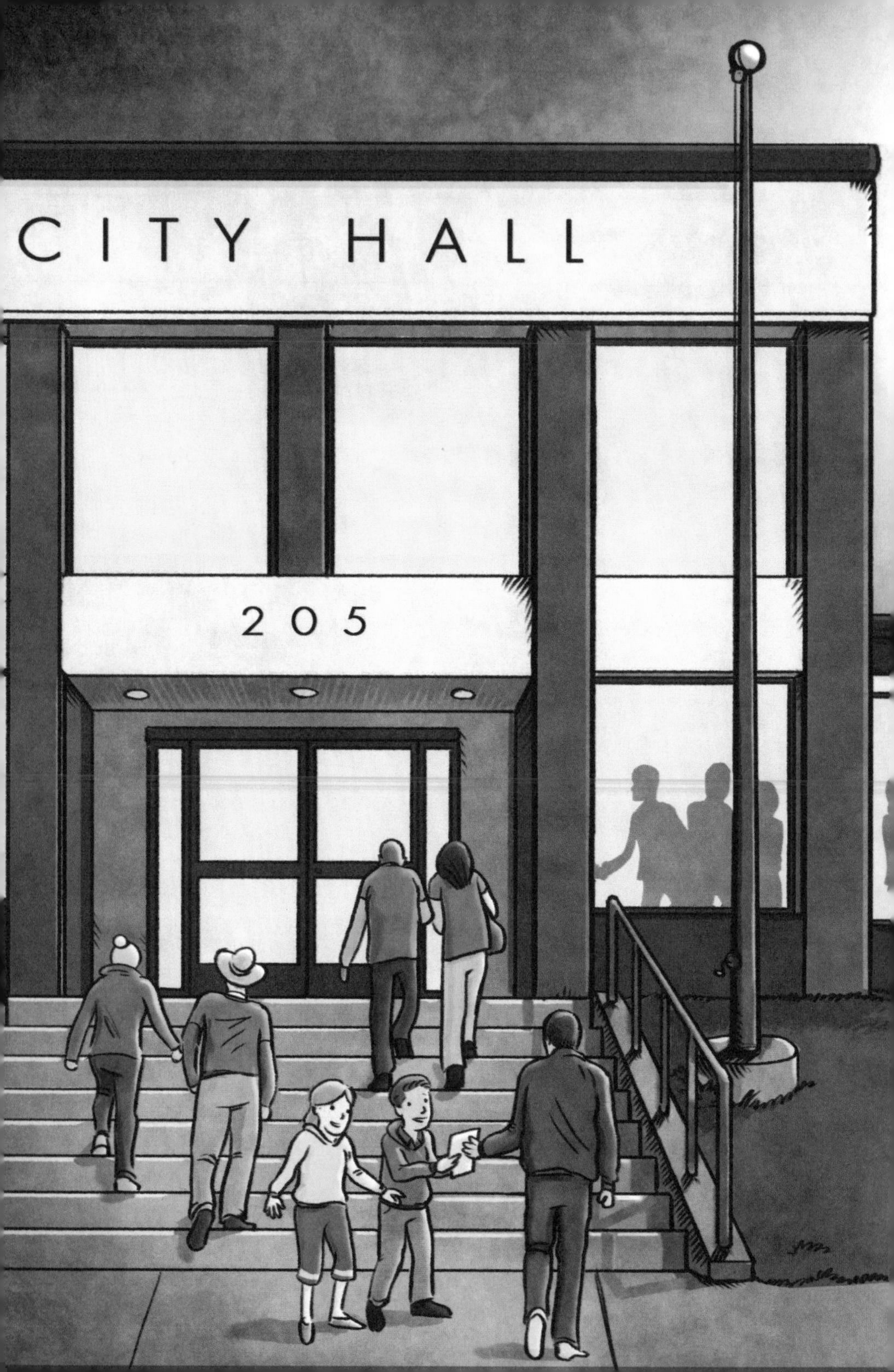
CITY HALL
205

The Tuttles weren't the only ones whose phones had been ringing nonstop. Food truck customers and others from the community had been calling the Mayor and city council members, upset that they would pass laws that let people like Bob shut down his competitors.

The following Tuesday night was the city council meeting, and the room was packed with reporters and people wearing green shirts and buttons.

During the public comment period, several food truck owners got up and explained how the unfair laws had hurt their business.

Pinky from the barbecue truck wanted to sell his food at a low price, but because of the regulations he wasn't allowed to. The regulations said his food couldn't be priced less than other restaurants.

The couple from Bang-Bang Noodles wanted to have their daughters help them work in the family business, but were afraid the police would fine them. One of the regulations said that only adults could work inside food trucks.

A man from Hoggie Burger felt thrilled to be a business owner, but couldn't make enough money to pay all the extra fees to the government.

The woman from the little taco truck found a great location where she wanted to sell food during the lunch hour, but was told she had to move to different places each day. Because of this law, her customers never knew where her food truck was.

Finally, the Tuttle twins approached the podium.

"My brother and I have a lemonade stand," Emily told the elected officials. "We'd be pretty upset if we had to follow all of these extra rules."

"We've learned that many of the laws and rules that businesses have to follow are used to help big companies hurt their competition. These are called protectionist laws," Ethan added, reading his notes.

"And that's what the laws on this paper are," he said, holding up the list of food truck regulations. "It's not fair, so it has to stop. You need to repeal them and treat these businesses fairly, like any other restaurant."

Regulations
for Portable Food Vendors

1. NO PFV MAY OPERATE IN RESIDENTIAL AREAS.
2. ALL PFV MUST OBTAIN A SPECIAL PFV PERMIT.
3. ALL PFV MUST OBTAIN A SPECIAL LICENCE.
4. ALL PFV WORKERS MUST OBTAIN SPECIAL CERTIFICATIONS.
5. NO PFV MAY OPERATE AT A LOCATION LONGER THAN 8 HOURS.
6. NEW LOCATIONS MUST BE APPROVED BY LOCATION SERVICES.
7. $350 QUARTERLY LOCATION APPROVAL SERVICE FEE
8. PRICES MUST REMAIN WITHIN 20% OF COMPETATIVE AVG.
   WORKERS MUST BE OVER THE AGE OF 18 YEARS.
   ...OR MUST BE APPROVED BY PFV COMMITEE.
   ...DE A COMMERCIAL SIZED SINK.
   ...Y OF PRODUCT.
   ...TABLES.

The Mayor and council members looked really embarrassed. Now everyone knew what had happened, and how the Mayor and Bob had hurt these businesses.

The Mayor wanted to avoid the news reporters and not say anything, so after the council voted to repeal the unfair food truck laws, he ended the meeting and quickly left.

Cheers erupted throughout the building, and food truck owners rushed around Ethan and Emily to congratulate and thank them for saving their businesses. Jared and Amy lifted them into the air in celebration. The crowd worked its way outside where there was a special surprise!

Mr. and Mrs. Tuttle had set up the twins' lemonade stand outside City Hall, where a long line of customers eagerly awaited them!

"Three cheers for the Tuttle twins!" Amy shouted, as the crowd raised their glasses of lemonade to celebrate the hard work and accomplishment of Ethan and Emily.

The End

The Author

Connor Boyack is president of Libertas Institute, a free market think tank in Utah. He is also president of The Association for Teaching Kids Economics, an organization that provides teachers with educational materials and lesson plans to teach economic ideas to their students in a fun and memorable way. Connor is the author of over a dozen books.

A California native and Brigham Young University graduate, Connor currently resides in Lehi, Utah, with his wife and two children.

The Illustrator

Elijah Stanfield is owner of Red House Motion Imaging, a media production company in Washington.

A longtime student of Austrian economics, history, and the classical liberal philosophy, Elijah has dedicated much of his time and energy to promoting the ideas of free markets and individual liberty. Some of his more notable works include producing eight videos in support of Ron Paul's 2012 presidential candidacy. He currently resides in Richland, Washington, with his wife April and their six children.

Contact us at TuttleTwins.com!

Hi, parents!
I'm Henry Hazlitt.

The book in your hands is packed with several important lessons, each of which deal with the study of economics. I discuss these principles in more detail in my book, *Economics in One Lesson*.

This field of study is haunted by more fallacies than any other—and it's no accident. Unlike subjects such as physics, math, or medicine, the subject of economics is complicated by the pursuit of selfish interests—people "gaming" the system to gain power or wealth over others through force or fraud.

Throughout history, governments have attempted to redistribute wealth and intervene in the economy, when they should merely encourage and preserve a free market. Competitive disadvantages are created by unjust laws unfairly giving preference to some businesses over others.

When Alexander the Great visited the philosopher Diogenes and asked whether he could do anything for him, Diogenes is said to have replied: "Yes, stand a little less between me and the sun." It is what every citizen is entitled to ask of his government.

My book is a thorough analysis of this unfortunate trend. Your children have been introduced to the key ideas in my book—and you, as a parent, will no doubt have countless real-world examples of the protectionism these fictional food trucks faced.

In my day, government interference in the economy often took the form of manipulating the production and pricing of commodities like wheat, raisins, and milk.

In your day, government imposes barriers that prevent innovative upstarts from competing against established industries—Uber and Lyft fighting to compete against taxis, Airbnb trying to compete against the hotel industry, and yes, food trucks trying to legally operate while restaurants use the government to shut them down.

The future of the free market depends on both understanding, and fighting, the protectionism that runs rampant throughout government.

To that end, please consider picking up a copy of my book to learn more!

Glossary of Terms

Capital: Also referred to as "financial capital," this is money that a person uses to buy or create something, in order to sell it and profit from the investment.

Competition: The attempt to win something by being better than others who are doing the same thing.

Profit: The difference between what something costs and what somebody paid for that thing; a financial gain.

Protectionism: Shielding one business or industry from competition by others using taxes or regulations.

Regulation: A rule established and enforced by government.

Discussion Questions

1. Why are established businesses tempted to support laws that punish their competitors?
2. Isn't it okay for a business to protect itself from competition?
3. Should a city council be limited as to what regulations or laws it can require people to obey?
4. Why does competition result in better or less expensive goods and services?
5. Was it important for the twins to raise awareness of the problem caused by the food truck regulations?

Don't Forget the Activity Workbook!

Visit **TuttleTwins.com/FoodWorkbook** to download the PDF and provide your children with all sorts of activities to reinforce the lessons they learned in the book!